THE CANADIAN
CONDITION

THE CANADIAN CONDITION

CONDITION

Reflections of a "Pure Cotton"

Henry Mintzberg

Stoddart

Published in 1995 by
Stoddart Publishing Co. Limited
34 Lesmill Road
Toronto, Canada
M3B 2T6
Tel. (416) 445-3333
Fax (416) 445-5967

Stoddart Books are available for bulk purchase for sales
promotions, premiums, fundraising, and seminars. For details,
contact the **Special Sales Department** at the above address

French edition, *Les propos d'un "pur coton"*,
published in 1995 by Québec/Amérique

ISBN 0-7737-5775-9

Cover Design: the boy 100
Printed and bound in Canada

*Stoddart Publishing gratefully acknowledges the support of the
Canada Council, the Ontario Ministry of Citizenship, Culture,
and Recreation, Ontario Arts Council, and Ontario Publishing Centre
in the development of writing and publishing in Canada.*

Contents

Preface

This is one of the fastest books I have ever done, and one of the slowest. I had been developing a series of articles for the newspapers, when suddenly I realized I had too much material, and it might make a small book. That was sometime in May, and the book appears in September. (I'm used to weightier books that take five or ten years to write and a year to produce.)

Yet these ideas have been mulling around in my mind for years. How could anyone possibly live in this country these past twenty-five years and not think about the "Canadian condition"? I have never published anything on political issues. I have stuck to management and organization. But I was asked to give a speech at Queen's University in January of 1992, as part of the celebration of their 150th anniversary. They asked me to speak on management, but management did not seem all that important right then. So I presented a paper called "Some Fresh Air for Canada." A number of the ideas developed here were first expressed there. But you could really say that these ideas have been developing throughout my life.

I am an academic who can produce scholarly papers like the rest of them. This is not one such example. This book is a personal statement — a "polemic" in the traditional, and, I hope, positive, sense of the term, a labour of love concerning the people and places I care deeply about. Montreal is a vibrant, exciting, and honest city; Quebec is the home of the nicest people I know on earth; Canada, in its quiet way, is one of the great countries of the world. Why give any of this up?

We would all do well to step back and take a different look at ourselves. It is in this hope that I have written this book. It is a little book with a big purpose.

~

Bill was wonderful. Bill Litwack has been a dear friend for an awfully long time. He took this book by the horns, fought with me viciously over every comma and concept he didn't like, and didn't let go until I fixed it. Thank goodness it's over.

Elana Trager ran around digging up the most obscure source material, from who taxes beer in Canada to when Charles de Gaulle first crossed the Atlantic Ocean. She never knew what was coming next, but she never flinched. Nor did Kate Maguire, who knew all too well what was coming next. You see before you five chapters; with all the writing and revising, for Kate there were closer to fifty chapters. Thank heaven for both of you.

I got lucky with publishers, too. Two very professional houses committed to a difficult schedule, and with great enthusiasm. I am deeply indebted to Jacques Fortin and Jean Straehl of Québec/Amérique and to Nelson Doucet and Don Bastian of Stoddart. Jean undertook the translation with great professional seriousness, while Don turned the manuscript around with remarkable speed and many helpful comments.

I must also thank Harvey Schachter for his advice, Ginnette Lamontagne for a number of helpful comments, and Henri Tremblay for those friendly arguments, as well as Jonathan Story for taking me more seriously than I took myself.

Now, if you expect me to say that despite all of this help, I am solely responsible for what follows, forget it. We are all responsible for what follows, all 28,000,000 of us.

HENRY MINTZBERG
Lac Castor
July 1995

"Pure laine" is the label used by those Québécois and other French Canadians who like to trace their origins back to the days of New France. All the rest of us immigrants — non-French-speaking, as well as French-speaking who arrived after 1760 — might, therefore, call ourselves "pure cotton." Except, of course, for the "pure furs," who arrived long before the rest of us.

~

And so:
This book is dedicated
to the pure blend
that constitutes the fabric of Canada today.
May our problems
continue to sustain our success.

I

Our "Distinct" Similarities

I am a Québécois — "pure cotton." I was born in Quebec, raised in Quebec, and have made my career in Quebec. I have a colleague named Donald Savoie who is not a Québécois. He is Acadian, born and raised in New Brunswick, where he has made his career. But he is "pure laine." In that respect, we are different. But in many other respects, we are rather alike: we are both academics, we both write books and give speeches, we even think alike on some important issues. Language and ethnic origin may matter for purposes of classification, but not for everything.

Of course, all of us like to focus on whatever makes us distinct, often magnifying our differences with any reference group that happens to be handy. In a threatening, insecure world, this seems to offer the comfort of an identity. But at a price. Some years ago, in an experiment, a third-grade teacher told her class that "blue-eyed people are better than brown-eyed people." The result, in her words: "I watched wonderful, thoughtful children turn into nasty, vicious, discriminating little third-graders."*

In fact, the blue-eyed kids *were* different, at least in one respect. So what? Imagine a New Guinean bushman being dropped onto the streets of Montreal and being asked to distinguish an anglophone businessman from a francophone sociologist. Would the fact that they might consider each other so different impress him? (The bushman would probably find it easier to distinguish the sociologist from a forest worker in Lac St. Jean.) Is this all a matter of identity or of insecurity? Pride or prejudice? Take your pick. Better still, pick them all.

We are myopic in this country, inclined to see everything too close up. As we focus on our differences, we become blind to our similarities. My

---

* Quote from "A Class Divided," aired on *Frontline*, Show #309G, WGBH Educational Foundation, May 30, 1995, a revisit of the 1970 ABC News documentary "The Eye of the Storm."

favourite example occurred a few years ago, during the Oka crisis, when a visiting British friend reacted with incredulity to something she saw on television. A native, who to her looked and sounded like a perfectly normal English Canadian, was being interviewed. At one point, he referred to the CBC interviewer of obviously Asian extraction as "you whites"!

Of course, there are all kinds of obvious differences, some even significant, between people who speak English, French, Cree, and Inuktitut. I live in Montreal precisely because of such things. It is a rare privilege to be part of a mixed society, where people can benefit from their differences without losing their distinctiveness. But we hear enough about these differences in this country; I think it's time we gave more attention to our similarities.

~

Let me begin with that contentious issue of the "distinct society." Why did the proposal that Quebec be recognized as a distinct society meet with so much resistance outside Quebec? Part of it was no doubt a kind of bloodyminded reaction: why "them" and not "us"? (Always them and us, those nice, neat, racist categories.) But much of it was not: to many people, something just didn't feel right about the formulation. I may be a Québécois, yet no one would identify me (or a million other Québécois "pure cottons") with that distinct society. But can anyone honestly deny membership in that distinct society to Donald Savoie — "pure laine" though not Québécois?

Quebec is a political jurisdiction, not a distinct society. Borders do not make a society, people do. French-speaking Canadians, wherever they may live, form that distinct society, which is precisely how René Lévesque first described it: "Le Canada français est une nation véritable," he told a *Le Devoir* reporter on July 5, 1963.

This is not to deny Quebec as the focal point of that society, nor the critical role that its government has to play in supporting and protecting it (which Lévesque also made clear in his 1963 interview). Rather, it is to challenge the all-too-convenient omission of one million members of that society who live outside Quebec. This point has certainly been made before. But that does not make it any less germane today, not if people are to take precedence over politics. In the words of Donald Savoie, who is a professor at the University of Moncton, "provincializing" language and culture threatens the "very existence" of the non-Quebec francophones, despite the recent advances they have made in preserving their rights.* (Savoie did not take kindly to references by Lévesque and others to his million compatriots as "warm bodies," nor to the comment by Parti Québécois cabinet minister Bernard Landry that they would be invited to move to a new, sovereign Quebec. Savoie pointed out that the many fishermen and farmers among them are hardly mobile.)

Defining distinct societies by people instead of place is more inclusive not only of all French-speaking Canadians, but in fact of all Canadians. In that sense, it provides an honest and equitable way to describe the Canadian situation, and so to help put aside the acrimonious "why them and not us" argument. Canada is a country of three founding peoples: the aboriginal peoples who first inhabited the land, the French-speaking people who followed, and the English-speaking people who followed them. If a society is "distinct" only in reference to others — you can't be distinct in a vacuum — then the English-speaking Canadians, the "pure cottons," form a second distinct society, and the aboriginal peoples, the "pure furs," form a third. In effect, by origin or else by adoption, all of us belong to one or

---

* From the article "Don't Sacrifice Francophones Outside Quebec for Unity," published in the Ottawa *Citizen*, among other newspapers, January 13, 1992.

other of three distinct societies in this country.

How distinct really are each of these "societies"? I cannot imagine anyone seriously questioning the distinctiveness of the French-Canadian culture in Canada. But are English-speaking Canadians all that distinct a group? Compared with the French-speaking Canadians, it may not seem so. Certainly the differences from a Newfoundland on one end of the country to a British Columbia on the other are vast. But there can be distinctiveness amidst differences (as is true for French-speaking Canadians, too).

A country develops to protect what matters to its peoples. If the protection of linguistic culture is important to one group, then that group has to be equally tolerant of whatever form of protection is considered important by other groups. In one particular respect, most English-speaking Canadians across the country find themselves distinct and wish to preserve that distinctiveness. This is with reference to the Americans, and American values, attitudes, and culture. English Canadians believe their society stands as an important alternative to the enormously influential American lifestyle. They feel that Canada demonstrates to the world that it is possible to be North American, with all of the obvious benefits that entails, without being American, with all the obvious problems. As evidence, they point to the historical stream of American immigrants, from the United Empire Loyalists to the Vietnam draft dodgers, who came here in search of that other North American lifestyle and stayed to reinforce and help shape it.

And what of the distinctiveness of that third "society"? The better question might well be: Are the English- and French-speaking people all that different from each other compared with the aboriginal peoples? Are common law and civil law really so different when compared with traditional native forms of justice? How about English and French cuisines (Cheddar cheese versus Brie? Apple pie versus tarte au sucre?) compared with the traditional native diets?

In fact, the Indians and the Inuit, whom I have lumped together based on common problems, historically have been far more different from each other than the British have been from the French. While those latter two were repeatedly crossing that narrow channel between their countries — to mate as well as to fight — the Indians and Inuit sat on either side of a less precise but in many ways more formidable barrier: the tree line. This created vast differences in every conceivable aspect of life: social organization, custom, dress, transportation, shelter, and defence, not to mention language itself.

The weaving of these three societies into the fabric of this country should be reflected in its constitution, to help ensure their protection and preservation. But we also need to transcend these obvious differences, not only to avoid discrimination, but also to recognize that many of our critical problems cut across cultural and language groupings, problems such as economic development, bureaucracy, poverty, crime, and debt. They must be dealt with collectively, if they are not to swamp us separately.

~

What especially distinguishes our three distinct societies is their fundamental similarity. Each, in a certain respect, is distinct in exactly the same way. All three define themselves by external threat — they share a common siege mentality. The source of the threat may differ, but not the fact of threat itself. The French are threatened by the English. The English are threatened by the Americans. And the aboriginal peoples are threatened by all of the above. It is the perfectly Canadian way to behave, on the fear that the masses will overwhelm our vulnerable little group. We understand each other so well in this country precisely because we spend so much time talking past each other.

But when we stop talking, what has been our typical response? We huddle together, like a herd of muskox. We close ranks against the world, even when we get angry at each other. (Well, that's not really true, because we generally let our leaders get angry for us. On a day-to-day, person-to-person basis, we actually get along remarkably well.)

By so closing ranks, and reinforcing each other's fears, we actually protect each other. Quebec indépendantistes would hardly agree (there is not much they would agree with in this book), but I think there is a case to be made that English-speaking Canadians, with their own fears of American cultural domination, have actually helped to buffer francophone culture from outside forces. Likewise, the aboriginal peoples of Canada have had to deal with much less of a melting pot in Canada than have their counterparts in the United States. And the example of a rich and vibrant francophone culture right in their own backyard has certainly not hindered the English-Canadian quest for distinctiveness from the Americans.

What our distinct societies really do is define each other. How could we possibly imagine any of them without the others? Where would they possibly be without the "bloody French," the "maudits anglais," and "you whites" against which to define themselves? Thus, we have achieved a nice, steady, protective balance in this country. We need each other for self-preservation as well as for self-identification. This is undoubtedly one of the powerful forces that have held us together all these years.

But it is not the only one. We have a great deal more in common than just our obvious differences. Let me try an even trickier issue: race. One can hardly dispute the racial distinctiveness of the native peoples, compared with those of European descent. But how about those Europeans themselves, especially the French and British settlers?

Would I dare to question the differences between Latins and Anglo-Saxons? Not exactly. I know about the stereotypes — fun-loving emotion versus rational fair play, and all the rest. What I am less sure about is the application of those labels. How Anglo-Saxon are the "pure cottons" and how Latin are the "pure laine"?

Many French Canadians trace their origins to Brittany and Normandy. Significant numbers of English Canadians do so to Ireland and Scotland. In that case, maybe we are dealing here with sizable numbers of francophones and anglophones of the same racial stock, namely Celtic. A Celt, according to Webster's Dictionary, is "an individual of any of various Celtic-speaking peoples, including the ancient Gauls and Britons and the modern Irish, Scots, Welsh, and Bretons."

Maybe all those trips across the English Channel erased what has appeared to be the deepest difference of them all. The people on both sides apparently spoke the same language back in ancient Greek times. They might have carried all kinds of behaviours and habits across, reinforced later by the significant mixing of the Irish and the French right here. For example, some of Quebec's best-known dishes — tourtière, ragoût de pattes et de boulettes, and tarte au sucre — find their equivalents today not on the French side of the Channel, but on the English (as Mme. Benoît, the dean of Quebec cuisine, liked to point out). So might it be that under the skin, deep in our irrelevant veins, many of us truly "pure laine" and "pure cottons" (well, not me exactly) come from the same line? (Ironically, the term "pure laine" might originate from the English expression "pure line.")

The implication of all this could well be profound: our real fabric might be Viyella! But that's not bad: it's a classy blend, in fact, combining the softness of cotton with the warmth of wool. How appropriate! Even if it does take some extra effort to maintain.

But until someone develops a test to prove what

ethnic blood really does flow in our veins, or that we really are what we eat, we might better direct our attention to how we behave today, rather than to who our ancestors slept and ate with yesterday. And in this regard, I find no shortage of significant similarities. Just take a step back, or, better still, out, and you will see what I mean.

~

What I believe characterizes most people in Canada today — whatever their "distinct society" — is a certain low-key, friendly tolerance. Yes, tolerance. Despite all the wrangling, Canada remains a very tolerant place from coast to coast. (Or should I say, there is all this wrangling because Canada is such a tolerant place.) Indeed, we are who we are precisely because of this.

Whoever complains in Canada gets the attention. The Americans confront; the Canadians comply. Someone I know — Québécois by adoption, francophone by language — tells it this way: The American says: "*Hey!* Get off my car!" The Canadian says: "Get off my car . . . eh?"

Compare Canadians of all cultures with people in our favourite reference countries, and we generally come out as less aggressive than the Americans, less class conscious than the British, and less arrogant than the French. In other words, we are a rather more tolerant people. These are stereotypes, to be sure, but I believe they do reflect a good deal of real behaviour, more or less. These three countries have histories of rather aggressive foreign policy; we, in contrast, have developed our reputation as peace-keepers.

Take a trip abroad and all this becomes clearer. You find that Canadians, French- and English-speaking alike, generally have a worldwide reputation for that low-key tolerance — as tourists, businesspeople, diplomats, and soldiers. In other lands, even Britain and France, you find that English Canadians and French Canadians just don't seem all that different from each other.

Indeed, perhaps the real distinction in Canada today is not between the languages people speak but between the vast majority of Canadians, in each of our distinct societies, who share these traits of tolerance and good will, and others, in all three societies, who would stir up racial tensions. For, unlike most multilingual countries, such as Belgium and the former Yugoslavia, our tensions exist largely at the political, rather than the individual, level. It bears repeating that on a personal level we mostly get along just fine. (I was involved in the creation and administration of a joint doctoral program in management among the four Montreal universities, two anglophone, two francophone. Whatever frictions did arise were mostly more serious between the universities of the same language.)

Maybe the real reason to salute the flag in this country is that it is one of the few places in the world where nobody expects you to. We have never managed to confuse a piece of cloth with human dignity. Tolerance has meant respect for Canadians of all stripes, not for Canada. If someone feels more Québécois than Canadian, or more Montréalais than Québécois, who cares, so long as human dignity is respected. Of course, we can take this only so far. Canada has to survive, too, if the desirable traits engendered by its existence are to survive.

I see this trait of tolerance in my own work as a professor of management. I believe, for example, that it is reflected in a characteristically Canadian style of management. (Ironically, after I first wrote this, I came across an article on a style of management rather similar to this, except that there it was described as Québécois!*) Some years ago, I chaired a "Canadian deans panel" at a conference. It turned

---

* Alain Chanlat and Renée Bédard, "Managing in the Quebec Style: Originality and Vulnerability," *International Studies of Management and Organization*, xxi:3, 1991. See especially pp. 27 and 28.

out that the deans of the Harvard Business School, Stanford Business School, and London (England) Business School were all Canadian. A coincidence? Maybe. Or maybe a reflection of our nature. Who better to manage prima donna academics than tolerant, low-key Canadians?

Right across the country, we have the most collegial universities I have encountered anywhere. They are certainly a lot less hierarchical than the British, a lot less politicized than the French, and a lot less pressured than the American. And this seems to extend to the management of professionals in general. To paraphrase Winston Churchill, we may well have the worst system of health care in the world, except for all the alternatives. It is certainly far less divided by class and ability to pay than those of the United States, England, and France.

And why is it that both Montreal and Toronto house some of the largest engineering consulting firms in the world? Might we have a competitive advantage in the management of professionals? Professionals prefer low-key tolerance in their managers, and we have that — in spades. A chief executive of one of the major Canadian transportation firms once said to me, "We can't run trucking companies worth a damn in this country." Sure — that takes a real S.O.B. Maybe we should leave it to the Americans (while we run their health care?).

Another trait we share is our attitude toward government, very different from the Americans. When any problem arises in this country, our natural instinct is to turn to government, demanding that it *do* something. Don't be fooled by the latest anti-government trends coming in from the United States. We retain this almost obsessional belief that government will solve every problem — providing better medical care, more pollution control, stronger cultural institutions, and so on. The level of government that the people of our different distinct societies turn to may vary — federal for many English Canadians, provincial for many French Canadians, local (band councils) for many of the aboriginal peoples — but not the fact of turning to government. Just look at the monumental investment we have made in constitutional talks in this country, almost all of it by government officials.

~

So look where I end up. I started by criticizing people who overemphasize their distinctiveness and I finish by overemphasizing our distinctiveness as Canadians. But I believe I have good reason: to help us see past our obvious internal differences to our less evident strengths. And to help ensure that we don't lose those abundant strengths by allowing the country to break up. We need Canada to preserve the Canadian way of life.

Maybe, then, it is time for us to acclaim our distinct similarities — the very things that make us unusual, and interesting, when you think about it. For these are what help to define as well as to protect our distinctiveness, not only as a nation, but as cultural societies within that nation, and especially as individual human beings within that. We have had enough of pure polyester, thank-you — enough of isolating that which is synthetic, artificial. It is time to celebrate our unique blend of natural materials.

II

There Is No "Rest of Canada"

There is Canada. There is no "rest of Canada." The country is made up of a number of political jurisdictions. Take away that big one called Quebec and you end up with four small provinces on one side and five big ones as well as two territories on the other. The fact that they share the English language no more ensures their acting as a single entity than did the fact that the two parts of Pakistan after the Indian partition shared the Muslim religion.

People from the "rest of Canada" share one other thing: a resentment of references to the "rest of

Canada." When Péquiste Bernard Landry used the term on television a few years ago, Pat Carney, the former Conservative minister from British Columbia, called it "patronizing to us." Her comment was perfectly understandable, for the term takes an immense range of people spread across thousands of miles of geography and lumps them into one nice neat category, based on the language they happen to speak. That may reflect the perspective of M. Landry's party, but it does an injustice to the reality of the country.

It also does an injustice to history. Three founding peoples — the aboriginal peoples, the French, and the English — opened up every part of the land. When the Europeans first arrived, the aboriginal peoples were already spread throughout the country. Indeed, the Europeans used aboriginal names for many places in the country, including Quebec, Ontario, Manitoba, Saskatchewan, and Canada itself. Montreal may be a name derived from French, but the island had an aboriginal settlement for thousands of years before the French arrived.* (The city may be older than Rome!)

When the French and the English came, both spread across the entire expanse of the territory.

* "Where Was Hochelaga?" *Canadian Geographic*, November-December 1994, p. 68.

That is why we still have a town called Fleur de Lys in Newfoundland and a Lac La Biche in Alberta, as well as cities called Sherbrooke and Valleyfield in Quebec. On either side of Chaleur Bay in the mouth of the St. Lawrence River, we find the towns of New Carlisle, Hopetown, and Kelly (just down from Shigawake), facing Maisonnette, Bas Caraquet, and Petite-Rivière-de-l'Îsle (just up from Shippegan). But the former are on the Quebec Gaspé side while the latter are in New Brunswick. Before we got into the habit of putting everyone into those convenient geographical boxes, things were all nicely mixed up through our history. (Indeed, the first apparent written reference to Toronto, another Indian name, was "Lac de Taronto," on a map of 1680 attributed to a French official. Later the French "Fort Toronto" was built on the current site of the city — "a proper place for a factory," a writer from New England said a short time later.*)

By now, of course, there has been considerable consolidation, reinforced partly by natural population shifts and partly by efforts — on all sides — to reinforce those narrow boxes. But French-speaking communities continue to exist all over the country, including major ones in Ontario and New

* "The Real Story of How Toronto Got Its Name," *Canadian Geographic*, September/October 1994 p. 68.

Brunswick, and even several small ones in western Prince Edward Island, while remnants of long-established English-speaking communities remain active in several corners of Quebec. The aboriginal peoples, of course, maintain communities throughout the country. Add to all of this the immense variety of other ethnic groups that help to constitute the entire country and you end up with the real Canada today.

It may serve some political agendas, and not only in Quebec, to encourage people to continue consolidating themselves into those boxes. But that will not necessarily serve the people themselves. Everything we have built in this country — and it is considerable — we built together. This includes the fur trade at the outset and the canals and railroads that followed, as well as some of our great accomplishments of more recent times, including one of the world's great expositions, Expo 67. These were not just English or French initiatives, but cooperative ones. We have also developed a remarkably effective and bilingual federal civil service — the envy of many nations — which has given us one of the most respected medical and social welfare systems in the world. All of this may not always have been easy, especially across different language and cultural groups, but we would do well to judge the results of our efforts and not the process of getting to them.

~

Of course, distinguishing Quebec from the "rest of Canada" is a way to foster the mindset of separation. But it is also a way to be lured into a possible trap. For if the idea can be implanted in people's minds, so, too, can the assumption that with independence will come the simple matter of negotiating some sort of agreement with the "rest of Canada." Politicians from Quebec will simply sit down with their counterparts in Ottawa and work it all out. Business as usual — just with different passports. Thus, Clause 2 of the spring 1995 "Draft Bill on the Sovereignty of Quebec" — after a Clause 1 that claims, rather prematurely, that "Quebec is a sovereign country" — reads: "The Government is authorized to conclude, with the Government of Canada, an agreement the purpose of which is to maintain an economic association between Quebec and Canada."

So simple.

Let's leave aside the fact that the current head of the Canadian government comes from Quebec, and, in the event of a Quebec declaration of independence, that he would soon give way to some tough nut from English-speaking Canada. (Quebec indépendantistes who formed their image of English-Canadian politicians during the leadership of Lester

Pearson or Joe Clark would be in for a nasty surprise. That great Canadian tolerance would disappear as fast as the federation.) Let's also leave aside the obvious point that if political negotiations among the provinces have proved so difficult within Canada, how can anyone expect them to be easier outside it? Let us just ask politicians who have been so concerned about their own power to give some thought to the power of others.

Which provincial premier would defer to Ottawa? "Sure, Mr. Chrétien [or whoever], please feel free to negotiate on our behalf. As premier of Alberta, I, Ralph Klein, have full faith in Ottawa. As always. After all, are we not all happy members of this new country called 'The Rest of Canada'?"

The notion that one province will unilaterally declare its independence and then the other nine will line up obediently behind an emasculated federal government would be nothing more than laughable if certain powerful people in Quebec politics did not claim to take it seriously (in the hope that others in Quebec will do so). What it constitutes, therefore, is a dangerous, and potentially tragic, fallacy.

The immediate effect of a Quebec declaration of independence would be to isolate the Atlantic provinces and embolden the western ones. Provinces such as Alberta would make it clear from the outset that Ottawa would never negotiate on their behalf, and the others would likely follow suit. So, at best, Quebec would find itself negotiating, not with Ottawa, but with as many as nine other political entities. I say "at best" because I don't think many of them would negotiate at all, not about economic association.

What incentive would Alberta or British Columbia have to reach a trade agreement with Quebec? At present, they may be perfectly (or imperfectly) happy to maintain what has been built up over a century in Canada. But once that's gone, what in the world would encourage them to renew it? I refer here not to bloodymindedness (though there would be no shortage of that in certain quarters) but to sheer economic pressures. As the respected economist (and friend of Quebec) Tom Courchene has pointed out in his book *In Praise of Renewed Federalism*,* it may simply not be in their interests to come to an economic agreement with Quebec. All four western provinces, whose combined population exceeds that of Quebec, would likely look more pointedly south, not east.

---

* Issued as part of *The Canadian Round: A Series on the Economics of Constitutional Renewal*, edited by John McCallum and published by the C. D. Howe Institute in July 1991.

Well, that's okay, a Péquiste might respond, because the real player for Quebec is Ontario. And "it is in their best interest" to reach an economic agreement, as we have been told time and time again. In other words, Quebecers will make a highly emotional decision and English Canadians will react with cold-blooded objectivity. As usual. But this is another of the great myths of the independence movement in Quebec. If you believe it, then I suggest you think again. Better still — *feel*. Feel as others might feel, for it is a feeling that might turn out to be all too familiar.

It is hard to believe that it is in Quebec's best economic interests to remove itself from one of the wealthiest countries on earth. Yet that is what Quebecers are being asked to do. This is, after all, supposed to be a question of culture, pride, emotion. Well, no single group has a monopoly on those sentiments.

Anyone who wants to see emotion in this country might try busting it up. Nationalist sentiment in Quebec might well prove to have been tame by comparison. For the most highly emotional people are often those who have always been so carefully rational. They keep their emotions in check so long and so tightly that when these finally blow, all hell breaks loose. Then those who have usually been the emotional ones just stand there dumbfounded, asking in perfect innocence: "What in the world happened?"

Nowhere is Canadian nationalism stronger than in Ontario. And so, nowhere else would anger over the breakup of the nation be greater. I believe that, in the event of a Quebec separation, Ontario would refuse to negotiate seriously. Or, more to the point, no politician in Ontario would dare sign his or her name to an economic agreement with an independent Quebec. Not for years, not until long after any serious agreement would remain possible. You can't repeatedly play chicken with someone and always expect him to be the one to move aside. One day he won't, and then you had better be able to get out of the way. If Quebec has just taken a "damn the consequences" decision, is it not conceivable that Ontario may well be prepared to do the same thing? And given its industrial base already tied closely to the U.S., why not? The consequences would be far less severe than in Quebec.

Well, then, Quebec would simply turn to the United States, too. Why not? Except for one small detail. The "rest of Canada" would exist in one strict sense: all the international trade agreements would continue to hold. But Quebec, newly outside of Canada, would not be party to such agreements. They would all have to be negotiated. A recent report by the Quebec government "Sécretariat à la restructuration" has claimed that this would be no big deal. But one might instead wish to heed the words of the United States ambassador to Canada, who said, on January 25, 1995: "This is a complicated legal question which would take a great deal of time to resolve and is certainly not automatic." Moreover, many Americans have deep personal ties to people in places like Ontario and Alberta, and it is hard to imagine any U.S. government reaching agreement with Quebec before the other provinces do, or over the other provinces' objections. The Americans know their markets, and there would be a lot more customers in the nine remaining provinces than in Quebec. How long would Quebecers wait for such a trade agreement? How long could they? (And even if they did reach agreement with the Americans eventually, what would have been the point? Does a society of seven million people protect its culture by throwing its economic lot in with a far more aggressive culture of a quarter of a billion people?)

So Quebec might well be on its own, or else find itself left with only the Atlantic provinces. It is hard to believe that Newfoundland would act differently than Alberta or Ontario. But the other three provinces might do so, given their backs against the wall, or at least the sea. An independent Quebec might thus end up in an economic association with the three maritime provinces — with a combined population a fraction of its own.

A word on sovereignty-association — sugar-coated association applied to the pill of sovereignty — is appropriate here, since this has once again been brought out of the political medicine cabinet, this time by Lucien Bouchard, and swallowed whole by the previously reluctant Jacques Parizeau. That option remains just about as clear as it was when first described by René Lévesque:

> The more I thought about this project, the more it seemed logical and easy to articulate. Its main lines were beautifully simple and there was a paradoxical added advantage that was far from revolutionary. In fact, it was almost banal, for here and there throughout the world it had served to draw together people who, while determined to be masters in their own house, had found it worthwhile to enter into associations of various kinds with others. So association it was to be, a concept that had figured for a long time in our own vocabulary and a word that would marry well with sovereignty, sovereignty-association making a euphonious

pair. . . . [Independence, on the other hand, had acquired] an absolute, rigid character from demonstration to demonstration as if independence were an end in itself, that the name was not much more, alas, than an invitation to the riot squad! Like the rose, however, wouldn't it smell as sweet by any other name?*

Sovereignty-association, by whatever label, is not an option but a smokescreen, designed to coax enough Quebecers to vote for independence. It merely takes for granted what is neither probable nor likely even possible. Except that now, according to the current magical formula, the "rest of Canada" happily accepts association and then quietly takes its seats in some new political council alongside Quebec, in equal numbers. By some leap of imagination, it is assumed that leaving Canada would provide Quebec with more bargaining chips than staying inside! One is hard pressed to sort out the naiveté from the sheer desperation in all this. Imagine Ontario, with one and one half times the population of Quebec (a Quebec that has just split Canada in two), accepting half the number of seats. They'll love that in Sault Ste. Marie.

* René Lévesque, *Memoirs*, translated by Philip Stratford (Toronto: McClelland and Stewart, 1986), p. 214.

The indépendantiste politicians of Quebec have no trouble declaring what they expect from the "rest of Canada." If only they could be so articulate about what they would be able to offer in return. These imagined political negotiations thus take on a kind of "Lucien in Wonderland" character, with one side sitting at the table shouting its demands to the silence of the empty chairs on the other side. But maybe that is what we should expect from people who cannot see past the "rest of Canada."

~

There does remain one last card in the Péquiste deck, according to the rhetoric of its leaders. The debt. If the "rest of Canada" won't negotiate an economic agreement, Quebec simply won't negotiate on the debt. The PQ Minister of Finance made the astonishing statement, on February 7, 1995, that Quebec might not assume its share of the debt if doing so would undermine the new country's economic development. (Maybe someone should tell him that it already undermines economic development in the existing country. "It's not our debt," he added, "it's Canada's debt," which gave me a terrific idea. After Quebec does this, each province should follow in succession, so to speak, with the same claim, until only Prince Edward Island is left in

Canada — with a debt load I estimate to be something like five million dollars per man, woman, and child. Then PEI declares bankruptcy, and, issuing a great sigh of relief, we all get along with our own independent plans for economic development.) The Minister of Finance's colleague, the Minister for Restructuring, expressed another thought: Quebec's share is 18.5%, he claimed. "If the federal government refuses what we offer, it will wind up with nothing." That's his idea of negotiating. But the premier of Quebec sees it a bit differently. No, that's not true, he said in response to his finance minister's statement. Quebec will pay eventually. It's just that "the cheques will leave a little later."*

The other nine provinces of Canada would have no legal or moral obligation to negotiate an economic association with an independent Quebec. As already noted, some would have no economic incentive to do so either. But Quebec would certainly have an obligation, both legal and moral, to assume some part of the debt. To use one as a threat over the other is not only unconscionable but also dangerous, both for Quebec's reputation abroad and for its situation at home.

---

* Quotes from the Montreal *Gazette*, February 7, February 28, and February 7, 1995.

Let me be specific. On *the day* Quebecers would stop paying federal income tax, if the cheques for the debt did not come, the tax burden on other Canadians would increase substantially. An oilman in Alberta would be told that because President Parizeau has not got around to writing the cheques, his taxes have just increased by several thousand dollars a year. For a factory worker in Ontario, it might be several hundred dollars. How do you think they might react? Bear in mind that while all of this is now hypothetical, in that situation of extreme disruption and emotional intensity it could be explosive.

We are a civilized people here in Canada, about as civilized as other human beings, with about the same veneer of civilization. But we should have no illusions that this veneer cannot be ripped off by the basest elements in society, all ready to move in when there is disruption in people's daily lives. And with emotional levels high, such people are all too often supported by larger numbers of people prepared to suspend critical judgment, especially when encouraged by the irresponsible statements of their leaders. That is how a tolerant society can suddenly turn intolerant. Anyone who believes we lack any of these ingredients in English- or French-speaking Canada might consider the state of Ste. Catherine

Street after the Canadiens last won the Stanley Cup, or that famous flag incident in Brockville, Ontario, or an arena full of Péquistes who gave convicted FLQ terrorist Jacques Rose a standing ovation in 1981.

~

The people of Quebec face a knife edge. On one side is a Quebec that would slide to separation from a "rest of Canada" that might continue to exist in name only. That would be full separation — cultural, linguistic, geographic, political, *and* economic. Everyone ends up in his or her box. Jacques Parizeau gets his Quebec passport and his colleagues get to sit at the United Nations. But who will be left to "eat cake" in the cafés of rue St. Denis?

On the other side is a Quebec that remains in Canada, continuing to share one passport as well as all the other benefits and difficulties that have become so characteristically Canadian over the years. Except that, with some real commitment, perhaps a number of the difficulties could be addressed in a constructive, cooperative way. We can call this "de facto sovereignty-association," because, in a sense, that is what Canadian federalism really is: protection of language and culture with strong economic ties. But no separate passports.

Not available is the position right on the knife edge, the one with the hyphens, the associations, and the promises. Quebecers cannot have the cake of Quebec independence while being able to eat the economic consequences of the Canadian federation. That would rip Quebec society apart, as it would the myth called the "rest of Canada."

III

Decentralization Means Centralization

Years ago I did a workshop on organization with government administrators in Canberra, Australia. One of the participants — he headed the Great Barrier Reef Maritime Commission — blurted out at one point: "You talk about all these 'bureaucracies,' and 'adhocracies.' You left one out." "What's that?" I asked. "Hypo-cracy," he said, referring to people who talk about one form of organizing while actually enforcing another. He had a specific example in mind, which he knew all too well: governments that centralize in the name of decentralization.

When a government claims that it is about to decentralize, watch out. Some years ago, the government of Quebec announced a plan to decentralize the educational system. It was going to create regional authorities between itself and the school boards, and pass power to them. That was "decentralization." After all, the world is a vertical hierarchy, is it not, and power was going "down" it? But why this generosity? Because the ministry was having trouble controlling the school boards and hoped that regional authorities could do the job better. Thus, the real intention was not to push power down the hierarchy from the central ministry, but quite the opposite: to draw it up from the base. That is centralization, not decentralization: when power is drawn away from the many operating people who actually deliver the goods and services, in order to lodge it instead with the few administrators who are supposed to control them.

This confusion is not unique to Quebec. Every province in Canada — indeed, probably every political jurisdiction the world over — suffers from it. In fact, the first widespread use of the term "decentralization" in business described exactly the same thing. Alfred P. Sloan became famous for reorganizing General Motors in the 1920s. That was his great legacy. It came to be called "decentralization." But what Sloan really did was move GM in exactly the opposite direction. He took the set of independent businesses — Chevrolet, Buick, Oldsmobile, etc. — that had earlier been bought up to form the new company, and subjected them to the financial controls of a central headquarters, in order to rein them in. Sloan moved GM, relatively speaking, toward centralization.

Decentralization has to mean how *widely* power is shared in a system, not where it happens to be held. The issue is not about hierarchy — *devolution* of power down some abstract chart — but about the *dispersal* of power to various people. In the perfectly decentralized system, everybody shares power more or less equally, as in the old American town meeting or the newer Israeli kibbutz. In the totally centralized system, as is approached in highly dictatorial regimes, one person holds all the power. When, therefore, a few people control most of the power, due to their positions of administrative authority, that system has to be described as relatively centralized. (We could clear up a lot of these problems if only we could think beyond hierarchy. "Top" management, or managing in the "middle," are metaphors that often serve to distort our perceptions. We would do better to think of our leaders as coordinating from a "centre.")

By this token, the government of Canada has decentralized a great deal of power to the provinces over the years. But don't rush to praise its generosity. It had to do so. Canada is a federal state. The provinces simply exerted their political will. Indeed, constitutional power became balanced between these two levels of government thanks in great part to the perpetual and persuasive pull of Quebec, right from the establishment of Canada as a federal state in 1867. But the provincial level is where it stops, at least formally. Local governments have not received that kind of power. The Canadian provinces, unfortunately, are not themselves federal states. In effect, we have decentralized federally in order to centralize provincially.

Compare the distribution of power in Canada, or another federal state such as Switzerland, with that of England and France. The latter two countries have nearly twice the population of Canada, and many times that of Switzerland, yet are highly, and, from the perspective of most people in Canada and Switzerland, intolerably centralized. The French, for example, do not have to worry about "decentralized" regions in their educational system. French politicians have long prided themselves in the fact (or the myth) that at any given hour of any given day, every child of a certain age will have his or her schoolbook open to exactly the same page. The French Ministry of Education employs one million people: the paycheques of every single French public school teacher and university professor come straight from the central treasury. And England has one central health care system for all of its 48 million people. (Scotland, Wales, and Northern Ireland have their own systems.)

Now, when the Parti Québécois promises "decentralization" as a result of Quebec independence, I would not accuse them of "hypo-cracy." I believe their intentions are honest in this regard, even appropriate. What I would accuse them of is wishful thinking. I don't think they could deliver, or would even want to. It comes down to a question of power, not promises. I am not much of a believer in laws of human nature, except for one, Lord Acton's dictum: power really does tend to corrupt, and absolute power does corrupt absolutely. An independent Quebec would naturally lodge power in the hands of the administrators of one central government. As in England and France, there would be no constitutionally countervailing force.

~

Promises, especially ones that offer glory and salvation, come easily to politicians. They don't cost much — a few words, some pieces of paper. Action need only come later, and I know of no politician who has ever been put in jail for not delivering a promise. I do know of many who were not reelected. But sometimes that comes too late. We might all be in that famous lobster pot by then. And you can't uncook a lobster.

The "yes" side in any Quebec referendum has one great advantage. It can offer tomorrow's fantasies. Its job is to conjure up a glorious future and then sell it. Not to create it — that comes later — just to sell it. It is to its advantage, therefore, to promise everything it possibly can. The "no" side has a much trickier task. It must sell today's reality. Or else convince people of the dangers of tomorrow's fantasies. How do you write inspiring songs about that?

I recall an old comedy skit on a record my parents used to play. It was about the Bolsheviks, and it went something like this:

The speaker says: "Come the revolution, we will all be eating strawberries and cream." Someone shouts out from the audience: "But I don't like strawberries and cream." The speaker retorts: "Come the revolution, *you'll eat* strawberries and cream." Said the Parti Québécois cultural critic in 1991: "Once the people of Quebec take back their culture for themselves, their artists will not lack for financial support."* Get ready for strawberries and cream, all you artists. Then, in presenting his last budget, the Quebec Minister of Finance provided a lovely new twist: Don't give us independence in the referendum, and I promise your taxes will go up next time. No independence — *no more* strawberries and cream! No wonder a prominent leader in Quebec once said: "Few things irritate me as much as the fiery speech of the separatist promising us heaven and earth as soon as we become a republic." The speaker's name was René Lévesque and the year was 1963.[†]

The Parti Québécois promises two kinds of decentralization, one as a natural consequence of independence, the other to follow soon after. The first is that all political power will flow immediately to the government of Quebec. And the second is that this government will share it with the communities. Thus, in Section 3 of the recent "Draft Bill on the Sovereignty of Quebec," we find: "The constitution will provide for the decentralization of specific powers to local and regional authorities together with sufficient fiscal and financial resources for their exercise." But before you cash in those chips, ask yourself whether the government of an independent Quebec would have an incentive to deliver on that

---

* Quoted in *The Globe and Mail*, September 19, 1991.
[†] Interview in *Le Devoir*, July 5, 1963.

promise. And would it, itself, constitute a political system more decentralized than the one we now have? I think there is good reason to answer "no" to both questions. In fact, I believe we could well end up with far more centralized government than has ever been experienced in this part of the world.

In 1991, when the Arpin Report proposed that the government of Quebec take over all federal powers for culture and the arts and lodge them in a new super-ministry, there arose a rather unexpected form of opposition. A number of Quebec's own cultural groups — traditional hotbeds of nationalism — objected. For example, a group of twelve organizations of film and television artists "lamented the tendency of the government to direct activities in the cultural domain," while representatives of the music industry complained about the "dirigiste" spirit of the report. "Quebec does not have complete control of the management of *its* cultural programs," complained the report (italics added), as if a government must not only own the cultural activities of its citizens but must also exercise full control over them. The report stated that "the time has come to consider culture as an essential mission of the State. . . ." And so it must take the "leadership in cultural activities . . . conceiving and directing activities in the cultural domain." No wonder a representative of the

Quebec music industry responded: "There is no need for them to occupy a leadership role, for the simple reason that it is already occupied, by us."[*]

Beyond the artists' concerns about centralization, and about politicians who think it is their job to control individual creativity — that somehow artists have to be "managed" for the collective good — lies something else. Divided political power actually enhances individual liberty. In other words, constitutionally separated power, between two levels of government, breeds real decentralization. Leave things just the way they are, these arts groups seemed to be saying. We like the fact that there are two sources of support. By being able to play one off against the other, or just by being offered a choice, things become more flexible and thus more supportive of genuine creativity. Certainly francophone culture could not have suffered greatly from this division of power. Just look at what seven million people have accomplished (in comparison, say, with the fifty-five million people of France).

When the eminent Yale University political historian Paul Kennedy spoke at La Conférence de Montréal in June of 1995, he said: "By real

[*] Quotes respectively in *The Globe and Mail*, September 19, 1991, the Montreal *Gazette*, June 29, 1991, and *The Globe and Mail*, October 21, 1991.

sovereignty, we mean the chance to influence out-comes." Our current federalism may thus mean real sovereignty — for all of us. Interestingly, Kennedy contrasted the sadness of a Bratislava, a dead city in his view, with the vibrancy of an Edinburgh and a Barcelona. The first is the capital of the new and ail-ing breakaway Republic of Slovakia, while the other two are centres of strong cultural movements that have remained within broader political jurisdictions. In the case of these two cities, like the obviously equivalent case of Montreal, one is hard pressed to see how the absence of political sovereignty has dis-couraged *cultural* development. Indeed, the real effect may well have been exactly the opposite: cul-tures thrive not by being isolated politically and geographically but by functioning in eclectic societies.

~

My point is that federalism in Canada has been an inherently *decentralizing* force. By dividing powers, it has created conditions that enhance personal liberty. Governments that confront each other also keep each other in check; they correct each other's excesses. Where the federal government is remote, the provinces can get closer to the people. And when the provinces get carried away, the federal government can act as a balancing force. Places like France and England lack such mechanisms, and it shows, all too often.

Thus, numerous recent publications, really directed more toward business than government (but using the model of government), have sung the praises of federalism. James O'Toole and Warren Bennis, in an article entitled "Our Federalist Future: The Leadership Imperative," point out that "a true federal system is contractual and power cannot be rescinded unilaterally or arbitrarily." There is no "all commanding central authority which unilaterally delegates specific, limited powers to its subordinate units." Moreover, "the units are free to experiment and be self-governing to the extent they do not violate the fundamental principles necessary for the maintenance of the union."* More significantly, Charles Handy, the British management "guru," wrote in his book, *The Age of Unreason*:

> The philosophy of the federal organization is characterized by the word "subsidiarity." It is a word unfamiliar to most, but not to the adherents of the Roman Catholic Church where it has long been an established part of traditional doctrine. First enunciated by Pope Leo XIII . . .

---

* In *California Management Review*, Summer 1992, pp. 72-90.

the principle of subsidiarity holds that "it is an injustice, a grave evil and a disturbance of right order for a large and higher organization to arrogate to itself functions which can be performed efficiently by smaller and lower bodies." To steal people's decisions is wrong.

. . . Subsidiarity means giving away power. No one does that willingly in organizations, yet the federal organization will not work unless those in the center not only have to let go of some of their power but actually want to do so, because only then will they trust the new decision-makers to take the right decisions. . . .*

Surely it is no coincidence that many of the richest countries in the world, as well as those most renowned for their individual liberties, have true federalist structures — the United States, Canada, and Switzerland, for example. The United Kingdom and France are rather restrictive places with regard to freedom of information, the use of referenda, and class action suits. (Indeed, it was not long ago that the French government had an official list from which people had to choose their children's first names!)

---

* Charles Handy, *The Age of Unreason* (New York: Random House, 1991), p. 100.

Consider how medicare is run in Canada, compared with the National Health Service in England. The latter is one system for forty-eight million people, which over the years has functioned with a convoluted hierarchy of "Districts" within (at one time) "Areas" within "Regions." Canada, with about half the population, has not one medicare system but ten, held together by nothing more than a set of five guiding principles (that the service be "public," "comprehensive," "universal," "portable," and "accessible"). All of this is administered, I am told, by just twenty-two civil servants in Ottawa. So Prince Edward Island runs one medicare system for 130,000 people, while Quebec and Ontario run two others for seven and eleven million people respectively.

Let us stay with this example, because it helps to make a further point: that the problem with Canada is not too much federalism but not enough. Prince Edward Island actually spends less per capita on medicare than either Quebec or Ontario.* There may be several reasons for this (no big city, etc.). But one reason is certainly not economies of scale. It may very well be cheaper to run social systems for

---

* Figures for 1991 put PEI at $2140 per capita, Quebec $2282, and Ontario $2511. Source: *Health Facts*, Canadian Medical Association, May 1995.

small populations, where relationships are more inti-
mate and so controls can be more personalized
(meaning that people are less likely to cheat "the
system").

PEI gets to run its own medicare system. Cape
Breton, another island nearby, with the same population and twice the land mass, does not. Nor do
Laval, a smaller island (near Montreal), or the much
larger Vancouver Island, both with many times the
population of PEI. Why? Because by quirks of history, PEI happens to be a province, while the other
islands do not. Does that make Cape Breton Island
or Laval or Vancouver Island any less capable of run-
ning their own medicare systems? Not at all. It just
means that the provinces simply would not dream of
voluntarily giving up any of their powers. They are
not federal states.

In fact, consider how some of the provinces are
acting as they now find their medicare systems too
big to manage centrally. They "decentralize," just
like that educational system cited earlier. They are
setting up regional authorities to bring health care
costs under control (while England, incidentally, is
dismantling its regions — each side frantically seeking the answer in what the other is rejecting!). By
regionalizing, these provinces are not creating real
autonomy, but hierarchy, an intermediate level put

in place to look down on and control the people who actually deliver the service. In other words, they are adding to the bureaucracy, by taking power away from the people who actually practise health care and giving it to people who are supposed to manage them — most of whom have no first-hand experience in delivering the services, it should be added. Exactly what those Quebec artists were afraid of. Such administrators are wonderful at cutting costs, but not at developing systems that can maintain quality. They hack while the surgeons slice.

Why don't the provinces do unto others what has long been done unto them? Why don't they establish a few guiding principles (indeed, the very same five principles that now guide Ottawa), cut their ministry staffs to a couple dozen people, and then create a whole set of really decentralized mini-medicare systems with real autonomy? The provinces may have to maintain overall fiscal control of these services. But that need not be bureaucratic control. We have enough experience now of how Ottawa has exercised fiscal control, on one side, and how a tiny constituency like PEI has managed medicare, on the other.

~

A political jurisdiction doesn't need independence to grant independence to its people. Indeed, its own independence might very well discourage this by centralizing power in one place. A nationalist government in a new state of Quebec would pursue a nationalist agenda. That would encourage it to maintain close social and economic as well as cultural control. I find it difficult to think of the current leaders of the Quebec independence movement, such as Jacques Parizeau and Lucien Bouchard, as enthusiastic sharers of power. Indeed, the Parti Québécois has a record on this issue from its first mandate; maybe we should take a good look at this before accepting its promises.

But nationalism is not the real problem here. I would draw the same conclusion about any centralized state that lacks a compulsory mechanism for sharing power. Just consider how Margaret Thatcher — that great believer in decentralization, at least in principle — emasculated the local authorities of the U.K. for her own political advantage. Lord Acton's dictum is the issue here. Rephrased, it might read: those politicians with the most absolute power to begin with are the least likely to share it. And Acton said nothing about the language that power speaks — English, French, Russian, it's all the same. If we are to get some real decentralization of power in this country — to the local level — then I suspect that the federalism we have is far more likely to provide it than promises made for an independent and therefore not federalized state.

~

The term "renewed federalism" has generally been applied to a realignment of power between the federal and provincial governments, specifically increasing the power of the provinces. A brief glance at Canadian history suggests that there is no renewal in that; it amounts to more of the same — the old federalism. There has certainly been benefit in strengthening the provinces, especially the government of Quebec to help protect the francophone culture. But would more of the same further strengthen the francophone culture? The answer is not obvious. Indeed, those cultural groups in Quebec argued exactly the opposite. You do not protect a culture by building a wall around it. In today's world, you free it of the control of political and administrative forces. We should not forget that the object of a nationalist movement is not to maximize the power of its politicians but to protect the culture of its people.

We need more federalism in this country, but of another kind. We should truly "renew" a model that has worked well between two levels of government by applying it to a third. I prefer to call this "nested federalism." We need a constitutional means by which to pass certain powers to the level where they most concern us: where we live our daily lives, in our local communities. We do not receive our most essential services up in administrative offices, but down on the ground — in our schools, hospitals, civic centres, and so on, which have deep local roots. In other words, it is not the politicians or administrators who need to be empowered but the people: those who actually deliver the services and those who receive them. If we are going to create a new constitution, then let's do it to solve our new problems, not to rehash our old ones. And because these problems are hardly ours alone, we have a real opportunity here to lead the world in creative solutions.

Specifically, we need to ensure that we have the smallest delivery units possible, controlled as closely as possible by the recipients of the services — units with real autonomy, used in a fair and democratic manner. This does not mean a cessation of state functions in favour of market forces, as is now so popular south of our border. Rather, it means a devolution of many state services to the local level of government — the level closest to the recipients. And this, of course, is exactly the message conveyed by the PEI experience: that with the granting of constitutional authority, public power can be exercised efficiently on a small and personal scale. (Some people think even PEI may not go far enough. It is divided into five school districts, each serving an overall population of about 25,000 people. A fellow who used to run one of these districts told me that he thought they were too big! Maybe you have to be a civil servant in PEI even to notice.)

~

Quebec indépendantistes might respond that this kind of decentralization would threaten a vulnerable culture. I would disagree, on two counts. I do not believe the culture would be threatened, nor do I believe that it is so vulnerable. Call this the perspective of an insensitive "pure cotton," if you like, but I think not.

I belong to a minority, Judaism, that has long feared for its survival. When I was a kid, I listened to a rabbi go on and on about how threatened and vulnerable we were, about how tragic it was each time someone ate the wrong food or married the wrong person. Doom and gloom. I always wondered whether he was out to save the culture or to isolate it. Judaism experienced the slaughter of six million of its people, leaving behind twelve million, not a great many more than were killed. Yet it survived, and today, despite more intermarriage than ever, it remains strong and vibrant. And I believe this can no more be attributed to the presence of the state of Israel than can the vibrancy of the French-speaking culture in Canada be attributed to the state of France. They help, but most of us are doing fine far from their borders. There is much more to cultural survival than political power. Let's not confuse bureaucracy with pride and accomplishment.

The equivalent of those rabbis among the "pure laine" today — their purveyors of doom and gloom — are the people who point anxiously to Quebec's declining birth rate and a population of a mere seven million francophones in Canada. Well, *all* of Switzerland has a population of fewer than seven million, and its francophone proportion is lower than in Canada. This translates into a total francophone population not much greater than one million — hardly much more, in fact, than the Canadian francophone population *outside* Quebec. Yet those Swiss francophones form a proud, secure, and prosperous community within the Swiss state and would not dream of becoming French. (Switzerland, it should be noted, while less populous than Quebec and physically minuscule in comparison, is divided into twenty-six truly powerful cantons, averaging 260,000 people each. The biggest has just over a million people, and the smallest 14,000; five number under 50,000. There is even a Basle-country canton different from Basle-town! If we need a model of truly small federated political units that work, here it is — in what is probably the richest country on earth!)

~

It should be evident by now that I see another problem in this world, which may be the real threat to both collective cultures and individual liberties, and which I think gets lost in our whole obsessive debate about "renewed federalism." As someone who has spent a career studying organizations, I see it coming from organizing itself — from hierarchy and bureaucracy, remote and impersonal, from the suppression of individual expression and cultural variety in the name of institutional power. We live in a world of big, menacing organizations. They menace us as individual human beings and they menace our free cultural expression. The problem derives not only from big government, but equally from big business. There is much animosity toward governmental institutions these days. So we hear a great deal about "free enterprise" instead. But when the enterprises are truly free, the people are not.

The enemy, unfortunately, is not "them," but "us"

— each of us when we defer collectively and mindlessly to institutional forces. A bureaucrat is not some evil dumbbell in a suit. He or she is anyone who takes pat categories too seriously, who sees everything in the absolute blacks and whites of "us" and "them," "English" and "French," "left" and "right," "Quebec" and "the rest of Canada," "westerners" and "easterners." That makes us all bureaucrats of one sort of another. We set our categories, fix our borders, draw our lines, and then expect everything to be fine inside. It never is. There is no substitute for thinking things through for ourselves — not via some institutional affiliation or social identification, not collectively or culturally, not in any category, but individually, as you and as me.

Fortunately, we all have the capacity to resist those bureaucratic tendencies, too. We all recognize nuance, even if only to the extent of "some of my best friends" are "them." If we really want to deal with our problems, then we should start to resist an awful lot harder. It is time, in other words, for some real decentralization — in the state of our minds.

IV

"Look Out
Your Window!"

I hate bumper stickers. Thank goodness, they're mostly gone. But I would like to see a window sticker, just one, just for us, just now. It would go on home windows, car windows, shop windows, all sorts of windows.

There would be a blue maple leaf at one end, and a red fleur-de-lys at the other. In between, in English and French, the message would read: "Look out your window!" For if we spent less time in this country looking at television sets (where we get mad at "them") and more time looking out our windows (where we can appreciate "us"), we might all be a lot happier.

A few years ago, two Calgary professors named Bercuson and Cooper published a book called *Deconfederation: Canada without Quebec.** It was part of the so-called "bon voyage" argument, that the other nine provinces should happily let Quebec go. The authors complained about our "generation-long constitutional crisis, probably the longest-running constitutional crisis in the history of the world." Well, so what? Who cares? It did not seem to get in the way of these guys. Life is good in Calgary, is it not, despite all those horrible debates in Ottawa? Think of all the other mischief the politicians might have caused if they didn't have this constitutional crisis to keep them occupied. Who forces these professors to watch television anyway? "Hey, guys, look out your windows!"

During all this supposed hell, a United Nations report in 1992 looked at the quality of life in 160 nations and concluded that Canada ranked first. First! The study considered purchasing power (Canada was second after the United States), life span (Canada was among the highest in the world), education, and other factors. True, no mention was

---

* D. J. Bercuson and B. Cooper, *Deconfederation: Canada without Quebec* (Toronto: Key Porter Books, 1991).

made of having to watch constitutional debates on television or needing to read books on deconfederation; apparently these things did not receive much weight in the ratings. A few months later another report appeared, this one putting Montreal on top of the list of desirable cities of the world in which to live. So here you have it, at least if you believe such surveys: the best city and the best country (not bad ones anyway). Just so long as you keep your television set off. It was this, no doubt, that encouraged Josh Freed, a Montreal journalist who understands his country a lot better than the learned professors, to say on radio: "Canada works in practice; it just doesn't work in theory."

In Quebec, the quality of life on the streets may be among the best anywhere. But on the television sets, it has to be among the worst. For here, every time it rains, you have to watch Quebec politicians blaming it on Ottawa. It can get to you after a while.

I think it got to an old friend of mine. A francophone "pure laine" who learned English in the logging camps of Ontario, he is now retired from a successful career in a large corporation. He and his wife have a happy life in a town near Montreal, surrounded by all sorts of friends, anglophone and francophone.

I dropped in on him a few years ago to discover

that he, a staunch federalist all his life, had suddenly became an indépendantiste, on the day, he claimed, that Jean Chrétien was elected head of the Liberal Party. Somehow, after the defeat of Meech Lake, that to him was the ultimate insult.

Needless to say, our conversation heated up. "Look out your window," I kept saying. "Tell me how your own life has been affected by all this." But no, he kept referring to things he saw on that damned television set.

His wife sat quietly through most of this discussion, silently urging me on. A westerner by birth, and bilingual, this tolerant woman had little tolerance either for her husband's new-found nationalism or for some of the attitudes she had encountered in a recent trip back to her western hometown.

Even when the conversation got hot, our respect and affection for each other never waned. At one point he offered to show me an interesting passage from a book on how the southern Europeans might look to a Mediterranean union for cultural affairs and to the EEC for economic ones. As he walked to get it, I warned him about "aiding the enemy." He smiled and kept walking. He knew I wasn't the enemy. We ended the evening making plans to ski together, so we could argue some more. What better way for francophone and anglophone friends in this country to spend their time?

Later I thought to myself, he doesn't even need to look out his window. He lives the benefits of the Canadian union right in his own home. I don't like the metaphor of marriage for relations between English and French Canada. We are more like siblings who live together (although many of us are the progeny of the union of the two cultures). But for him and his wife, this is no metaphor. The warmth of their personal relationship contrasted sharply with the anger of his politics — a microcosm of political relationships in Canada today.

His argument was not with me, or his wife, or his kids, or his friends. Like the rest of us, he was angry with "them" — the ones he sees on the media. A couple of idiots stomp on a Quebec flag, or another fool suggests that children caught talking English in a Quebec schoolyard should be expelled, and millions of people boil. Imagine if we never heard this "news." Imagine if we all had to judge our lives by the things we live. People who stomp on flags don't represent English Canada any more than people who want to expel kids for speaking English represent French Canada. Yet my friend had converted distant political battles into a political position from which, were it to occur, he personally would lose a great deal in his everyday life.

~

English Canadians reacted to evident flaws they saw in the Meech Lake accord. And they supported Jean Chrétien's leadership, not to put French Canada in its place — that is an absurd notion — but because they felt (and still feel, as, apparently, do increasing numbers of Quebecers these days) a genuine affection for this man: finally, an authentic human being in high office. Not everything is image and posturing. People do sometimes respond honestly to what they feel, even if it may not be politically correct. But the nature of the media today is such that extreme positions get taken for public sentiment and so all sides get their backs up, hating people they never met while forgetting about those they know perfectly well.

We are rarely reminded of the many parents across English-speaking Canada who have been putting their children into French immersion classes, or of Quebec's long-standing support of English-language institutions. Nor do we hear much about quiet evenings in which friends argue respectfully in each other's respective languages.

What we did hear a great deal about were such ordeals as having to look at French on the corn flakes boxes and having to accept all those bilingual federal jobs out west. Well, go back and look at your cereal box and see how corn flakes has been translated into French. "Corn flakes"! Maybe we spend too much time reading the fine print in this country. And while you are at it, consider what proportion of federal jobs out west have been designated bilingual: all of 3% (though the proportion is much higher, and appropriately so, in places like Ontario and New Brunswick).

Those Calgary professors claimed in their book that "for most Canadians, the independence of Quebec poses no threat to anything." I think they are dead wrong. It may well pose a threat to almost everything we cherish in this country, in all parts of it.

~

The economic costs and benefits of separation have been debated ad nauseum. I find it hard to believe that anyone can still argue seriously that there would not be significantly higher costs. Certainly the short-term consequences would be enormous. And not just in Quebec.

In a recent paper entitled "Financial Options for a Country Wanting a Divorce," parts of which were published in *La Presse*,[*] Reuven Brenner argued that it would prove almost impossible to transfer to

---

[*] Working paper, Faculty of Management, McGill University, 1994, parts of which appeared in *La Presse*, January 18-19, 1995.

Quebec part of a debt that is now owed to Canada. Which lenders would entrust their money to a new, uncertain country, and at what interest rates? Canada would likely have to maintain Quebec's share of the debt, on its behalf, at some increased rate of interest, and the load could well prove crushing for both. "If [countries] do not have access to credit, sovereignty becomes a costly illusion," Brenner wrote. He concluded that from this point of view alone, Quebec could never afford to leave Canada — not if its people wished to maintain some semblance of their current lifestyle.

But we should not stay together just because we are stuck together. We should stay together because we have a great deal to celebrate together. Just look at what we have created in this country. Look at our style of life and our quality of life as well as our standard of living. Look at how we are rated by outsiders looking in. Look at the richness of the francophone culture, every bit of it developed within the Canadian federation.

As prime minister in 1905, Wilfrid Laurier claimed that "the twentieth century would be the century of Canada."* Today, those who even remember this comment must find it quaint: we have long

---

* Speech in the House of Commons, February 21, 1905.

---

since given up on that prediction. Yet those studies cited earlier suggest that Laurier may have been right after all. We just never noticed. We were all so busy looking for the usual indicators of success — political influence, economic and military might, diplomatic status, all those things you see played out on television every evening — that we lost sight of the ordinary, everyday things that make a place great. Right outside our own windows.

There is the story of a farmer on his deathbed who tells his children that there is a fortune in the field. If they dig, they will find it and get rich. And so, after he dies, they dig and they dig. They never find the fortune, but their digging improves the field and so they live comfortable lives.

We dig and we dig in this country, especially in the constitutional field. But we never quite find the fortune. Instead, we just improve things gradually, to the point where we have achieved our own comfortable lives. Let's not throw that away for some supposed fortune buried elsewhere.

Isn't it time we stopped getting annoyed at the abstractions we don't live and the extremists we don't know, and started celebrating the reality we do live and the friends we do know? Why don't we just turn off our television sets for a while and enjoy the view from our windows.

V

Some Fresh Air
for Canada

The words "constitution" and "compromise" are bundled together in this country as if they mean the same thing. But compromise is not the only way to deal with a difficult issue. Back in the 1920s, a clever American woman named Mary Parker Follett wrote what remain among the best words ever written on how to manage conflict. There are three basic ways, she claimed, two of which are flawed.

First is domination, "victory of one side over the other." The trouble with this is that the defeated side "will simply wait for its chance to dominate." Second is compromise, which "we understand well, for that is the way we settle most of our controversies — each side gives up a little in order to have peace." But that is hardly better: in "dominating, only one way gets what it wants; in compromise neither gets what it wants." Thus Follett suggested a third way, which she called "integration":

> Let me take . . . a very simple illustration. In a University library one day, in one of the smaller rooms, someone wanted the window open, I wanted it shut. We opened the window in the next room where no one was sitting. There was no compromise because we both got all we really wanted. For I did not want a closed room, I simply did not want the north wind to blow directly on me; and he, the man in the room with me, did not want that particular window open, he merely wanted more air in the room. Integration means finding a third way which will include both what A wishes and what B wishes, a way in which neither side has had to sacrifice anything.*

* Mary Parker Follett, *Freedom and Co-ordination: Lectures in Business Organization* (London: Management Publications Trust, published in 1949), pp. 65 and 66; Follet's work has recently been republished by the Harvard Business School Press as *Mary Parker Follett: Prophet of Management*, Pauline Graham (ed.), 1995.

Fresh air without the draft — what a lovely metaphor for Canada!

Domination has sometimes been used in this country, for example concerning the French schools of Manitoba years ago and the English signs of Quebec more recently. It has never been acceptable. Mostly, however, we Canadians have been the great compromisers. And this has often worked, more or less. But not in establishing a constitution. We tried to create one by domination, and when that resulted in the alienation of many people in Quebec, we tried to create two more by compromise. First, eleven people sat down at Meech Lake to divvy up our pie. That failed, alienating everyone. So the next time we gave every sort of self-declared interest a shot at it, and — guess what? — once more compromise, under the label of the Charlottetown accord, failed. The whole effort was summed up perfectly by an elderly neighbour of mine who has spent her life in a small Quebec town. Before the last vote, she remarked, "Peut-être il vaut mieux voter 'peut-être.'" ("Maybe it would be better to vote 'maybe.'") Then, on reflection, she added "C'est plus certain." ("It's more sure.")

Returning to Follett: "If we get only compromise, the conflict will come up again and again in some other form, for in compromise we give up part of our desire, and because we shall not be content to rest there, sometime we shall try to get the whole of our desire." Our one possibility, therefore — indeed our great opportunity — is her "third way": "when two desires are integrated."

Integration means moving the debate to another place, going back to basics to find a common ground. It "involves invention . . . and the clever thing is to recognize this and not to let one's thinking stay within the boundaries of two alternatives which are mutually exclusive. In other words, never let yourself be bullied by an either-or situation. . . . Find a third way."*

Integration means that all sides benefit — everyone gets at least what they expect, sometimes more, but not necessarily as they expect it. This is a difficult concept to grasp for people focused on their own power. Integration requires vision, and that is in short supply for those who are stuck in sibling rivalry — who have to run around everywhere proclaiming that "mine is bigger than yours" and that "I win because you lose." Put people with a little goodwill and some generosity in charge instead, then introduce a bit of imagination, and everyone can win.

---

* Quotes from "Constructive Conflict," in H. C. Metcalf and L. Urwick, *Dynamic Administration: The Collected Papers of Mary Parker Follett*, New York: Harper and Brothers, 1949, pp. 35, 32, 33.

The Queen's University economist Tom Courchene has commented on how "Canadians have displayed a rare genius in accommodating their political structures to internal and external forces." He added that "it is important to recognize that most of these innovations did not require a formal constitutional amendment, even though they affected the *de facto* division of power between Ottawa and the provinces."[*] But why can't we bring this genius to bear on the formal constitution as well? Why can't we convert this from an intractable problem into a rich opportunity — to create a constitution that could become the very model of how the modern nation state is able to govern itself.

In her essay on "constructive conflict," Follett begins with the argument that we should not "avoid conflict" but "use it . . . set it to work for us," much as the mechanical engineer, whose job is to eliminate friction, also capitalizes on it. Put friction to work, she tells us.

For us in Canada today, Follett's words are prophetic. "What people often mean by getting rid of conflict is getting rid of diversity," which is not the same thing. "We may wish to abolish conflict, but we cannot get rid of diversity." In fact, she

---

[*] T. J. Courchene, *In Praise of Renewed Federalism* (C. D. Howe Institute, 1991).

considers conflict a potential "sign of health, a prophecy of progress."

Her first step toward the constructive use of conflict is "to bring the differences into the open" so that they "can be clearly examined" — "viewed together and compared." This may stimulate integration as "a spontaneous flowing together of desire," often coming in "a moment when there is a simultaneous reevaluation of interests on both sides and unity precipitates itself." People who run workshops on collaborative processes like to use an exercise in which two groups are told that they both have dire need for a particular kind of orange. But there are not enough of these oranges left in the world for both. So they fight furiously over them — until they discover that one group needs the juice and the other needs the rind.

Follett proposes, as a second step, to "take the demands of both sides and break them into their constituent parts." Her advice here is particularly important for us. This "involves the examination of symbols, involves, that is, the careful scrutiny of the language used to see what it really means." To her, "all language is symbolic; but we should be always on our guard as to what is symbolized." We shouldn't get trapped by the wrong terms, Follett warns, pointing out "how often disagreement disappears when theorizing ends." One must "find the whole-demand, the real demand, which is being obscured by . . . minor claims or by ineffective presentation." Then the two sides must "prepare the way for response," bearing in mind that response has to be circular, not just sequential as in a game of tennis. I respond and you respond, to be sure, but "I respond, not only to you, but to the relation between you and me."[*]

~

If politics is the art of compromise, then our constitutional conflict may well be beyond politics — and beyond the politicians. (Could Follett of the 1920s possibly have foreseen Canada of 1992 when she wrote about the "mistake" of a chief executive who acts as an "arbitrator" instead of as an integrator?) Governments, as perceived by the Canadian population, "are intrinsically betrayers," said a psychiatrist who commented on television during the 1992 constitutional debates. But not intentionally. They betray only by default, exercising the wrong kind of leadership, particularly when what we need are creative solutions. But this should come as no surprise. We elect our politicians to reflect the popular will, not to be creative. That we end up with

[*] Follett, "Constructive Conflict," pp. 30, 31, 36, 38-39, 40, 41, 42, 45.

compromisers is perfectly understandable. The problem is just that under difficult circumstances, compromise does not work.

So, when the going gets tough, our regular leaders had better be going: they're not tough enough. Then we need integrative solutions and leaders with vision — people who have the foresight to appreciate new and unusual solutions, if not to invent them themselves, and the courage to champion them.

A visionary sees ahead — has an image of the future. But to see ahead, you have to be able to see behind: to have a deep appreciation of the history of a situation. You have to have lived it. Likewise, a visionary sees above — he or she sees that "big picture." But, again, to see above, you have to see below: to have a sense of the details, a profound understanding of the context. There is no vision from an ivory tower. And visionaries see beside: they see what other people haven't seen. These people don't resist popular tides; they ignore them. They create their own images and invest them with enormous energy; if successful, such images become the popular tides.

This means visionaries are tenacious, often obsessive people who tend to have little patience for the niceties of political life — all that diplomacy and compromising. You won't find them holding their fingers up to the wind, trying to figure out which way the opinion polls happen to be blowing. They do their own blowing.

Thus, don't look for visions in closed, smoke-filled rooms, nor in wide-open congressional conferences. Neither leaves much room for the fresh air to pass. If a visionary with an idea does sneak in, he or she is likely to be dismissed amidst all the posturing. People intent on sitting in the mainstream don't notice the side currents.

~

Was René Lévesque a visionary? Since I once co-authored an article entitled "Profiles of Strategic Vision: Lévesque and Iaccoca,"* I ought to have a ready answer. But the answer did not prove to be simple.

Lévesque had a dream for Quebec. But a dream is not a plan, and to realize his dream, he had to reduce it to a plan. And that is how he lost it.

Lévesque's dream, like most, was not very clear. Just go back and read his words quoted in Chapter 2 about sovereignty-association as that "euphonious

---

* Co-authored with Frances Westley, published in J. A. Conger, R. N. Kanungo, and associates (eds.), *Charismatic Leadership: The Illusive Factor in Organizational Effectiveness* (San Francisco: Jossey Bass, 1988).

pair." In the political process, the concept got converted into a strategy of "étapism" — nibbling instead of a big bite — which in turn came down to the wording of the question on a ballot, for the 1980 referendum. As the comedy team of Bowser and Blue put it in a song written this past July, fifteen years later (since these things seem to have a habit of repeating themselves): "It's not to be or not to be. The question is — what's the question?"* Lofty ideals were thus reduced to Cabinet fights over dashes and commas. And so Lévesque's vision went down to defeat, perhaps before the first vote was even cast.

Yet this revealed something else — maybe another vision — once the idea of sovereignty-association was peeled off. After the defeat of the 1980 referendum, when negotiations were renewed with the federal government, a rumour circulated in Lévesque's own Executive Council offices that he had reached a deal in Ottawa. Graham Fraser has described the scene:

> The reaction was pure visceral elation: cheers, hugs, shouts of joy. One senior civil servant who had once been a Parti Québécois official watched with a wry sense of discovery: even

---

* From "Into the Lobster Pot We Go," used by permission of George Bowser and Rick Blue, © You Guys Publishing, 1995.

there, even at the heart of the government's planning secretariat, the deep-rooted, fundamental desire was not for rupture and liberation from Canada — but for reconciliation.*

Better still, consider Lévesque's own words five years later, when he supported the position that the Parti Québécois should not contest the next election on sovereignty:

We have, in effect, for all intents and purposes, gone back to our roots. . . . That is to say that we are still, as we have been since the beginning, sovereigntists, but with the realism that the special situation that history and geography has made in Quebec demands. It is not for nothing that from the beginning, seventeen years ago, we evoked not only associate states, but even, do you remember, a sort of new Canadian community.†

Quebecers have been reluctant to let go of Canada, afraid, supposedly, of the economic consequences of separation. But might we have a better

* G. Fraser, *Réne Lévesque and the Parti Québécois in Power* (Toronto: Macmillan, 1984: p. 298).
† From the postscript added to the paperback edition of Fraser's book, 1985, p. 370.

reason here? Could it be that deep in their collective psyche, the "pure laine" of Quebec have a profound sense of being Canadian as well as Québécois? Might the long history, that natural blending, those distinct similarities be felt somewhere inside, even if hidden from the surface amidst all the emotion of "maître chez nous"? In 1985, the Parti Québécois government reinstated on the licence plates of Quebec the motto "Je me souviens" ("I remember"). Could it be that more is remembered than those Péquiste politicians had in mind? And while on the topic of remembering, we would do well to remember the words we just quoted from Follett: Get past the language, to find out "what is symbolized. . . . Find the whole-demand, the real demand." Has the real demand from Quebec been a plea for respect, pride, reconciliation? And, if so, could it be that René Lévesque proved to be a visionary after all — despite his own best efforts?

~

No such ambiguity surrounds Charles de Gaulle or his contribution to France. Vision works well when it matches the context. Moreover, ironically, in times of real crisis, when there is great confusion and too many people involved, visionaries work best by a kind of domination. But this is a domination willingly embraced by people, who recognize that only in one or a few fertile minds can the different needs be drawn together into an integrative solution.

Charles de Gaulle was not exactly a regular politician; he was dogmatic and difficult, a nuisance in the political process. But visionaries often are — they see only their own images. That is why they almost always get themselves rejected eventually.

Twice de Gaulle retreated from the political process. But the legacy he left France the second time has proved rather extraordinary. The vision he infused into the 1958 constitution has engendered the most stable period in the country's history, and the most prosperous by far. And all of this was accomplished in 120 days!

In the spring of 1958, France was in crisis over the fighting in Algeria. There was the real possibility of civil war at home. A reluctant National Assembly, stymied in its own timid attempts to rework the constitution of the Fourth Republic, turned power over to de Gaulle on June 1, 1958.

De Gaulle had a deep understanding of his own country, and a vision of what it needed in a constitution. This could be described as a kind of elected monarchy, hardly what we would accept in Canada, but well suited to a France prone to political stalemate. In fact, de Gaulle had articulated this vision in a speech he gave back in 1946. A small group around him worked his ideas into a proposal that was formally reviewed, first by a constitutional consultative committee and then by a state council, only some of whose relatively minor modifications de Gaulle accepted before the final document was published on September 5, 1958.

In the ensuing referendum, three weeks later, on September 28, a France that has always been far more divided politically than Canada has ever been linguistically, voted overwhelmingly for the proposal. A full 79% of the voters supported it, with the favourable vote not dropping below 64% in a single department.*

De Gaulle is long gone; in fact rejected by those same voters ten years later. But almost forty years after it was established, his vision lives on in a France made stable and prosperous in good part by that constitution (and, it should be added, upheld to the letter for the past fourteen years by the very same François Mitterrand who battled so vigorously against it in 1958). De Gaulle had no basis for

---

* A detailed account of the events surrounding the development and acceptance of the constitution of the Fifth Republic in France can be found in Roy C. Macridis and Bernard E. Brown, *The De Gaulle Republic: Quest for Unity* (Homewood, Illinois: The Dorsey Press, 1960).

vision in our world: he was seventy years old before he ever stepped foot on this side of the ocean, and, even then, he came to Canada only twice, briefly,* the second time to pronounce on its future. But, inadvertently, he may have rendered us a service by demonstrating in his own country that under difficult conditions everybody appreciates a sensible vision.

~

Are we capable of what Follett calls "integration" in this country? I believe so. Clearly there are people who prefer the opposite — separation — and others who would simply let them have it, who have been "bullied by [the] either-or." But the evidence seems clear that most Canadians, in all of our distinct societies, wish to preserve what we have created here. It is they who provide the potential for an integrative solution. Such a solution has to recognize the rights of single individuals and the preservation of collective identities as well as the needs of the nation state. It has to encourage pride without prejudice, fresh air without the drafts.

Let me sketch what some of the characteristics of such a constitution might look like in an ideal world.

* Michel Cazeneau and Olivier Germain Thomas, *Charles de Gaulle* (Paris: Éditions de l'Herne, 1973).

1. *We need a constitution that looks forward, not backward.* If we could get past our national obsessions, we could fashion a constitution that might well be the very model for the modern nation state. The United States constitution was once such a model; it hardly appears to be ideal for today's world, in which government has a critical role to play alongside the individual. We seem to have achieved a better balance between private liberties and public needs here in Canada; let's show it off in a constitution that helps to preserve it.

2. *We need a constitution that recognizes that we already have a constitution.* I refer here not to any formal document, but to over a century of working things out, one step at a time. We have no need for some great process of social reengineering. Such massive planning efforts all too often begin with lofty intentions only to end with empty wish lists — like a set of New Year's resolutions. Trying to work everything out at once, in principle, just evokes all kinds of irreconcilable disputes. Capturing instead in a document who we are, what we value, and how we have succeeded — a statement of pride in ourselves — can lead to the reconciliation of all kinds of

big problems in little ways: quiet, practical, integrative. We need to give full vent to that "rare genius" Tom Courchene wrote about, to deploy "more creatively" what he referred to as the "incredible variety of instruments" we have developed over the years.* Let's fix in our constitution only what is broke, not what ain't, to paraphrase that old saying.

3. *We need a positive constitution, not a negative one.* You don't write a constitution the way you sell fish in a market. You don't, as was done last time around, stick in a clause right near the beginning protecting the minority language rights of one group in one province, as if the others don't matter. A constitution should not be a set of "temporary compromises permitting the various forces to continue their warfare."† It should raise people's sights, bringing them into the fresh air, where there can be a spirit of constructive cooperation. Without that spirit, we would be wasting everyone's time even to try. That would just lead to more compromises and more divisiveness. We won't settle this by bargaining, not with any party that defines its

* Courchene, *op.cit.*, pp. 89, 87.
† Macridis and Brown, *op. cit.*, p. 118.

position as "more." But we needn't rush; we have our de facto constitution.

4. *We need a simple constitution.* The document should be succinct, to the point. Detail implies lack of goodwill. We need a constitution rooted in trust, conceived not to solve problems but to establish processes by which problems can be solved. In other words, we need a statement of principles that guides behaviour, not a specification of those behaviours themselves.

5. *We need a constitution for the people, not for the politicians or for the provinces.* This should not be an exercise in divvying up power among eleven governments. That is hardly the way to get an integrative solution. Under the guise of "renewed federalism," we get more of the same. We need a constitution that truly decentralizes, that allows power to pass to places where people can exercise it as directly as possible. The intention should not be to protect the provinces, or private property, or the federal state itself. Our need is not to reinforce bureaucracy, but to protect and uplift the people. To cite a Gaullist behaviour we can do without: "The conservative writer Jean Dutourd once described

Gaullism . . . as a refusal to confuse France with the French. The latter are the means, Dutourd wrote, France is the end, that is to say, a work for whose beauty no effort should be spared . . . "*
That is an abhorrent thought, a misplacement of basic human values. We need a constitution for Canadians, not for Canada.

6. *We need a constitution that expresses pride in our diversity.* To many French-speaking Canadians, this is a land of two nations; to many of the aboriginal peoples, it is a land of their nation as well; to many easterners and westerners, it is a land of diverse regions; and to everyone, it is a land of local communities. We have provincial governments that represent regional concerns and municipal governments that reflect local ones. We also need to recognize formally our three "distinct societies": English-speaking, French-speaking, and aboriginal. Quebec must play a special role in the protection of the French-speaking culture. And so must the aboriginal communities for the protection of their cultures.

---

* Richard Bernstein, *Fragile Glory*, New York: Knopf, 1990, p. 316.

7. *Finally, we need a constitution to stabilize relationships, not destabilize them.* It is time we faced a difficult issue. For those who want separation by referendum, a "yes" is a yes forever, while a "no" is a no for now. That enables them to keep coming back, time and time again. In Follett's words, we had better find another way. A minority of people have a right to express their wishes. But not at the expense of perpetual disruption for everyone else, including the majority in their own distinct society, to the point where everybody is worn down and just gives up. For then we may all have to find out the true cost of their intentions. But the cost of an endless series of "no's" can be high, too, as costly on the nerves as on the pocketbook. You have to leave this place for a few weeks and then return to realize how demoralizing all this is (with each side desperately seeking some outrage to exploit — another Brockville flag incident, another "Yvette scandal"), how sapping of energy that could be used for other purposes. (Unfortunately, you can't always escape even abroad. I was with my family in France during the 1980 referendum. When we heard the results, my eldest daughter, eleven at the time, asked, "Does that mean we don't talk

about it any more?" Sorry, Susie.) A constitution should designate when, under what circumstances, how, and how often such an issue can arise. It has to allow for self-expression without encouraging perpetual disruption. If Quebecers say no in the forthcoming referendum, we need to get on with other things.

Well! All that is a tall order. But maybe not impossible, not if we go about it constructively. I would love to close with *the* solution. Wrap it all up and go home so that I can gaze lovingly out my window. Finally be able to tell Susie that we don't have to talk about it any more. But no one can do that right now. What I can do here is suggest another way of approaching all this: indicate a process if not a product (really a process in the form of a product).

What follows grew out of a bit of whimsy on my part. If you permit me, I will maintain the whimsical tone. Serious matters are always treated far too seriously.

~

On the evening of the referendum on the Charlottetown accord in 1992, I was invited to dinner in Montreal. It was at the home of a rather suave couple, so I was not about to bring a box of chocolates. I

brought a constitution instead. I wrapped my constitution in red paper, put a blue bow on top, and
presented it to my "pure laine" hostess, with the
explanation that it was a serious effort because I had
spent the entire morning working on it. By the end
of the evening, I could at least claim that this was
the only unopposed constitution left in all of
Canada.

In it, I listed my qualifications for such an
endeavour: no knowledge whatsoever of constitutional affairs, never any involvement in politics,
some experience in synthesizing ideas into frame-
works, and a concern for country, province, and city,
but especially for the people who live in all these
places.

I should admit that I had some help. I had been
spending time at a business school in France called
INSEAD, and had become friendly with a political
scientist named Jonathan Story, a clever Englishman
who knows a great deal about constitutions. Of
course, as a good Brit, Jonathan believes that the
best constitution is no constitution. But he also
accepts that such documents are sometimes necessary — a "written constitution" as opposed to a
"living constitution," he said. The trick, of course, is
to have both — a written one that lives.

I consulted Jonathan about my intention on two

occasions, as I recall. He provided two bits of advice that stuck.

Keep it short, he insisted, ridiculing the 237 articles of the EEC "monstrosity" and the fact that the German constitution specifies who has the right to tax beer. (No problem about that in Canada.) We joked about getting it on one page. Details suggest lack of trust, Jonathan told me. You have to build a country on trust, rather than trying to develop specifications for an unpredictable future. A constitution should require people to work things out: it should encourage cooperation, not litigation.

Second, Jonathan stressed, a constitution needs a central concept, an inspiring idea that, in a word or a phrase, will attract the people by reflecting their national pride.

I share with you the results of my morning's work (which, I should acknowledge, has since been updated two or three times — involving at least another couple hours of work). Admittedly, it does not come to grips with all the needs listed above. But, most importantly, it can do so on a single sheet of paper (even if, when it got typed up, that required single spacing on both sides of the page). No serious country should have a constitution full of staples or paper clips or whatever. Some part of it might get separated. This is, after all, a document that is supposed to guide the lives of millions of people for centuries. What you want is a single page you can wave around — that you can show off to your German and other EEC friends.

There is still room on that sheet for a couple of the details I didn't get around to — like a sentence or two on secession, and another on the basis of sharing power among the three levels of government in a nested federation. Constitutional experts would insist that is the hard part. But if we could keep them out of it, as well as the politicians — you wouldn't ask the foxes to design the chickenhouse, would you? — then maybe developing some integrative solutions wouldn't prove all that difficult.

So here then, without further ado, is my modest contribution to the great Canadian debate. For all those politicians, notably provincial (so to speak), and especially from Quebec, who will, I am sure, be breaking down my door to express their gratitude, please note that chocolates will be fine. I'm not suave.

A Constitution
for Canadians

We have built a great nation in this vast and beauti-
ful northern land on the principle of tolerance. The
constitution of Canada is designed to promote and
protect that tolerance, for each and every one of
our citizens. We share a basic set of values in this
country, namely the wish to preserve and enhance a
cherished way of life: supportive of individual initia-
tive, comfortable economically, protective of cultural
diversity, and adaptive institutionally. This constitution
is deliberately brief, to reflect that tolerance. It specifies only basic principles, to provide a framework for
the constructive exploration of specific issues, which
must be the hallmark of every democratic state.

Every Canadian, regardless of origin, language, gen-
der, or other personal characteristic, is entitled to
live in freedom and dignity, subject to respect for
the freedom and dignity of others as well as of the
natural environment.

This is the principle of tolerance and it takes precedence over all that follows. In particular, institutions are important to our society, as is property, but both are subordinate to the preservation of individual freedom and dignity.

We are a nation of three founding societies, the aboriginal peoples who first settled this land, the French-speaking people who followed, and the English-speaking people who followed them.

This nation recognizes the need to protect and preserve its three distinct societies, with regard to language and culture, no matter where their people reside in its land.

In addition, we are also a nation of various regions, represented by the political jurisdictions of our provinces and territories. Moreover, we comprise a mosaic of diverse communities, of all sorts, deserving of continued respect. Political power in Canada is accordingly shared among three levels of government, federal, provincial, and local, determined according to national, regional, and community needs. Notwithstanding, in contemporary society the needs of the citizens are highly sensitive to the actions of established institutions. We therefore recognize a second level of federalism, between the provinces and the local jurisdictions, guided by the principle of decentralization, which specifies that

> Power over direct services to the public is to be devolved as closely as possible to the recipients of those services, namely to the smallest administrative unit and the most accessible political jurisdiction practical, subject to the values of fairness, consistency, and portability across regional, linguistic, and cultural groupings.

Nevertheless, we are one nation politically, and thus, under the principle of free exchange

> We are one nation for trade and commerce as well as for the practice of work, and so we are one nation for the rules that govern these.

We are, and shall continue to be, a nation governed by the body of precedent known as parliamentary democracy, adapted to our own needs in our federal parliament and the legislatures of each of our provinces and territories as well as in our system of courts.

This constitution recognizes the special nature of the French-speaking culture within Canada, and the fact that most of its members are located within the jurisdiction of Quebec. Likewise it recognizes the particular nature of the aboriginal cultures in communities spread across the country. Accordingly

The special, although not exclusive, role of the government of Quebec, as well as of the local jurisdictions of the aboriginal communities, is recognized in the preservation and protection of their respective cultures and languages.

While this constitution is meant to stimulate accommodation within a broad framework of general principles, amendments may occasionally become necessary. But they must be acceptable to the population at large as well as to the specific constituencies most affected, and must be considered so as to minimize disruption. Accordingly

Any amendment to this constitution, or fundamental change of its concomitant institutions or processes, must be proposed either jointly by the governing and the opposition party in the federal parliament or by provincial legislatures representing two-thirds of the population. It must then be approved in a national referendum, by majority vote in each of the country's four historical regions — Atlantic Canada, Lower Canada, Upper Canada, and Western Canada.

While emphasizing our domestic needs as Canadians, this constitution also recognizes our global responsibilities.

As members of the world community, Canadians are committed to the continued use of our influence and resources in support of the very values that we specify here for ourselves: the freedom and dignity of the individual, respect for cultural plurality, responsiveness of institutions, balanced prosperity, and peace and stable order.

~

My "pure laine" cycling partner used to like to remind me, especially when climbing some horrendous hill, that life is a journey, not a destination. But we always did manage to get to the top eventually, and then we would whiz down with great glee. Of course, another hill was usually waiting for us at the bottom. But when you are in good shape, and especially have the right attitude, going uphill becomes as much fun as going down. Certainly a lot better than staying home and watching television.

We have plenty of climbing left to do in this country. So we had better learn to appreciate it. But while we're at it, let's just slow down and stop puffing for a few minutes, and take a deep breath of that fresh air. Then have a good look around. Not bad . . . eh?

"The most important thing to remember about unity," Mary Parker Follett *pointed out, is "that there is no such thing. There is only unifying."*